8-90

A Short History

of the Long Ball

A Short History of the Long Ball

By Justin Cronin

Council Oak Books, Tulsa, Oklahoma

Council Oak Books
Tulsa, Oklahoma 74120

First edition
Library of Congress
  Catalog Card Number: 90-80294
ISBN 0-933031-23-8
Printed in the United States of America
Jacket and book design by Karen Slankard

8-90

For T,

and

in memory of my grandmother

Contents

Aerodynamics

When I was ten and Donny was twelve, I hit a ball that really sailed. I thought, as he pitched the ball to me: here is the one. It was a warm afternoon in late March, the dead grass lay in bleached tangles on the muddy earth, the sky, I recall, was a flat, featureless grey. The ball approached me, descending the backside of its lofty arc. Donny had meant for it to go high and outside, but instead had thrown a hitter's ball; it would drop straight to the plate, going slow, through the meaty center of the strike zone. As it neared, my sense of it —

my understanding of its ballness, I suppose — mysteriously amplified. I could feel its weight on the wood of my bat, the bottled energy of its rubbery core, and they seemed things detectable only by me, untapped wells of force in a cosmos of unseen forces. It was as if, eyeing that ball, I were peering into the future. I widened my stance, cocked my wrists neatly, shifted my center of gravity onto my back foot and prepared to greet the pitch with the full weight of my destiny. When we met, that ball and I, the world went crack and I felt a rightness, a stupendous rectitude that, in hindsight, I believe is reserved to revolutionaries, charismatics, some new parents and all hitters of the long ball. I spun clean around and as I spun at the top of my vision I saw it sailing up and away into the dark trees at the end of the meadow. I watched Donny watch it go over like a man watching a shooting star. We never did find that ball.

There were others we did find: brown baseballs with rotted seams, softballs half-frozen in cloudy puddles, thousands of tennis balls overthrown, overhit, forgotten: a king's ransom in balls. We rooted through those woods like archaeologists in a ruined cave, and when we found old balls, we found new ways to use them. We held pairs of them to our chests to embarrass our sisters, tucked them between our legs and waddled like tomcats, toted a load of them in the seats of our pants back to the house and ejected them, one by one, out the holes of our legs to roll across the kitchen floor. We threw them, waterlogged and heavier than they looked, at passing cars, at road signs, at dogs and at each other. The history of those days remains, in my mind, a history of recovered and lost balls.

The teams, the spring I hit the ball that sailed, were simple. There were my older sister Lucy and I, one team, there were our sometime neighbors Donny and Martha Flannigan, the other. The Flannigans lived in New York City, which at the time was a dangerous mystery to me (I rode the train in once a year with my grandmother to skate at Rockefeller Center, see the dinosaurs at the Natural History Museum and pick out a toy at Schwarz), and came out on weekends and for a month in summer. Many aspects of that family were variations on my own and inspired a confusion of bourgeois envy and Yankee distaste. Both our fathers were lawyers, but Mr. Flannigan was obviously a good deal better at it, or more ambitious, or simply a different sort of lawyer altogether. As a family they took lavish trips, drove expensive cars (a series of Jags occupied their driveway during the years I knew them), and once Mr. Flannigan defended a corrupt Bronx Borough Deputy Chief and had his handsome, square-jawed face on the cover of the *New York Post*. My father, round and thoroughly unhandsome, was a small-town lawyer and member of the County Board of Overseers; stalwart, thrifty and unflappable, disposed to pregnant moral silences, idle puttering and gizmos. His greatest love was sailing and on weekends he woke early to tack a catboat around the tame waters of Long Island Sound. I would be the first to admit we had money, but nowhere near as much as the Flannigans, who seemed to me glamorous and fabulously rich, closer by far than we to the beating heart that drove the world.

The Flannigans' house stood on the other side of the meadow behind our place. Mrs. Flannigan raised pulies — a mindless, yapping breed which even then I associated with the mania and indolence of city life — and they had bought the house as a sort of ersatz kennel, though I don't recall they ever had more than two or three dogs on the place at one time. The dog run stood out back and in summer, smelled like baking shit. On the trim above their front door a bronze plaque had been affixed, engraved with the date 1851 and a citation from the National Register of Historic Places. The previous owners had been a childless couple; the woman was a librarian at my school.

"I was mugged this week on the way home from the movies." Donny told this to me when we first met. I think I was eight. We were fooling around in the half-empty moving van parked in their driveway, trying to get to know one another, explaining the history of ourselves. It was cold and we could see our breath, which made me feel older. The air smelled of metal, burlap and grease.

"If I hadn't had a quarter to give him I'd be deader n'shit now. See?" He dug into the front pocket of his jeans, produced a quarter and flicked it cleanly to me in the dark compartment of the truck. I plucked it from the air and looked down at it with the admiration due an artifact.

"In the Big Apple, you never leave the house without a little something for the muggers," he explained. "And you keep it in a special pocket or something, so you can reach for it right off and don't have to give them your whole wallet."

Donny was two years older than I and much larger, with thick black hair, piercing blue eyes and angular, almost Oriental features. He was, for a ten year old boy, quite manly in his appearance. That he had looked Death straight in the face and bought him off with a quarter amounted in my mind to a studied accomplishment in defiance and cunning. His sense of the world seemed simply immense.

"That's a good idea," I said, returning the coin. "I wouldn't want to give my wallet to anybody. I carry a lot of personal stuff."

"Yeah?" Donny said. "Let's see." He extended his hand to receive my wallet, which of course was pure fiction. All the money I owned in the world — about five dollars in nickels, dimes and pennies and a few priceless-looking foreign coins given me by my grandmother — was stashed in a cast-iron fire hydrant on the top of my bureau.

I was doomed.

"Cough it up," Donny demanded.

"Well," I stammered, "I don't have it with me, right at the moment."

His upturned palm hovered in front of me, and at first I thought he had seen through my lie (I was too naive to see through his). But then he gave me a look of almost criminal complicity, a kind of gangsterish facial wink, and his hand fell to his side. I knew then that I had passed some kind of test, that Donny had joined me as a partner in my fib, and we were going to be friends.

"You're a cool one, you are." He knelt, took a pocketknife from his jacket and set about engraving his initials in one of the plywood beams that framed the truck's cargo compartment. "Maybe, when you get to know me, I can see it."

His sister Martha was a year younger than I and attended a girls' school of good reputation in the city. She was a shy girl with fine blonde hair who might have been pretty if not for the ugly scar at the corner of her mouth — the last trace of a burn sustained when, as an infant, Martha had crawled to an electric outlet (I see a blue carpet, apricot wallpaper, white cloth diapers swaddling her behind) and chewed the cord through to the wires. The skin on that side was faintly splotched — one might have mistaken this for shadows — and the scar, perhaps two inches long, tugged her mouth into a permanent pucker that afforded her face an attitude of great nostalgia and regret, as if she were looking back to the moment just before she had injured herself. When I met Martha, she was bouncing around the freshly hardened concrete of the dog run on a pogo stick and had already undergone plastic surgery twice; the third and final operation would take place when she was fourteen and her facial structure was complete. Despite her shyness, she possessed an athlete's body, boyish and lean, and enjoyed playing games.

My sister Lucy, one year my senior, also enjoyed games, though she was a reader and the activities she lobbied for were ambitious and bizarre. At school she had read a book called *Swallows and Amazons*, in which the children of two wealthy British families pass a summer between the wars chasing each other in small skiffs in a fantastically exaggerated game of nautical tag. In the process they discover a patrolling German U-boat and, through a complicated series of plot twists (I have since read the book — not bad really, though wildly implausible) prevent an invasion of their happy isles by the Evil German Empire.

Lucy suggested we apply the principle of *Swallows and Amazons* to land, and we did for a while — tearing after one another in the woods, plotting complicated strategies, zinging each other with rocks from high ground and treehouses — but the world at that time lacked easy enemies (we were uncertain who we were fighting in Vietnam, what the stakes were) and the maintenance of imagined global dangers quickly exhausted us. I had fallen in love with the Mets in '69, so when *Swallows and Amazons* limped into oblivion, we tried softball, and it stuck.

Here is how we played: Three bases, home, first and second. Two players in the field, one pitching, one fielding. An imaginary runner advanced in front of the actual. No strikes, no balls, everybody swung. A ball hit into the Petersons' yard (a disagreeable old couple who probably cared less about us than we thought) was irretrievable, frowned upon and a ground-rule double. Scores ran into the dozens; games ran entire afternoons.

Here is also how we played: with whoops and jeers (*Hey batter batter swiiiiing*), absurd derogatory rhymes (*we want a pitcher not a belly itcher*), with the absolute, tireless enthrallment of children who have latched onto a working solution to the problem of a boring world. In those days our bodies seemed to grow by inches overnight and could not be wholly trusted; our clumsiness was matched only by the grace with which we mastered space for an instant with a brave catch, a throw aimed and delivered on target, a hit made sweetly. My sister was weak, she was easily rattled at bat, and so when she came up to the plate we fell into an encouraging silence (I am still amazed by our generosity), knowing she would dribble no more than a single, if that. Donny hit the long ones, hard punching drives that could grab the web of your glove and yank it right off your hand. I was trained by the Pony League to hit grounders and line drives to the open field: schooled, sensible ball. Martha, it seemed, could hit anywhere she wanted, though not far.

The day I hit the ball that sailed, Donny had teased me. "You hit like a fag."

Incredibly, I didn't know what a fag was, except that it was something I didn't want to be. Striding to the plate, I said, "Fag this," and rapped a grounder to Martha, who took it on one bounce and threw it back to

Donny. It was a clean hit, but it didn't prove a thing. I didn't even bother to run.

"You see?" Donny said. He held the ball up, clutching it with two fingers and a thick, grimy thumb. Behind me, I heard my sister giggle. I sort of despised her, but in most things she was an effective emotional barometer. Her giggling confirmed my opinion that Donny was mocking me. "You see? No, you don't," he said.

Angry, I thought: what don't I see? It was a softball. I stepped out of the box and took a couple of practice swings — pumping my wrists like Willie Stargell, whom I admired — smeared my hands and the grip of the bat with dirt and spit. Pure theater. I stepped back into the box. The plate was literally that: a paper plate.

"Pitch it again," I said.

Donny held the ball aloft like a teacher waiting for students to identify oceans and continents on a globe. "I'm not gonna do anything until you tell me what this is."

"For Christsakes, it's a softball, all right? It's a softball."

"And what are you gonna do with it?"

"I'm going take your stupid head off with it, is what I'm going to do."

Donny looked at the ball and then at me. His face glowed with arrogance. "Better."

I burned. "Clean off. You'll bleed. A lot. But that won't matter because you'll be dead."

"Just pitch it," Martha yelled from the out-field. She had been waiting in a crouch, her hands cupping her knees. I didn't want to look at her.

"I think you're going to whiff, is what I think. Wiffer!"

I locked my eyes on the seams. "I hate you," I said, and he pitched the ball.

Silver Lake

hen I was a sophomore in college, I came home for Christmas and heard that Donny was in the rehab at Silver Lake. What my mother told me — dramatizing her story with a series of progressively diminutive clippings from the New York and Stamford papers — was that Donny had wolfed a snowbank of cocaine up his nose and raced his father's Jag off a pier into Long Island Sound. Donny had crawled out a window as the vehicle sank in six feet of water. A fifteen year old girl was snatched from the passenger seat by onlookers and

13

revived by CPR. Donny had gone into convulsions on the dock while they worked on the girl, his heart beating itself into a frenzy and stopping cold, to be restarted in the ambulance by electric shocks. Later at his hearing he had spat at the magistrate, the assistant district attorney and a member of his father's firm who was representing him. He had to be restrained by the bailiff and when that failed to calm him he was removed from the courtroom, to have his fate decided in his absence — a terrible thing, I felt, to be absented from the proceedings, almost as terrible, though in a different way, as his crimes.

I had not seen Donny for five years, and it seemed the right thing to do to go and see him now. I drove the thirty miles up to Silver Lake in an airy, blowing snow. The place was a converted Victorian mansion on a chalk bluff overlooking the Hudson. From the outside, it appeared the only architectural concessions made to its function were a high chain fence and a white shingled guard house at the end of the long drive. So far so good, I thought, I can do this. But inside was a different story. The structure had been gutted and its original finery replaced with what, I supposed, were the traditional appointments of a mental hospital: metal casement windows wired with alarms, muffling carpets, soothing ferns and bland, mahogany furniture. In the reception area, a pretty blonde nurse stood behind a long linoleum counter with a sign that said: "Visitors Please Register." I told her I had come to visit a friend in the Chemical Dependency Unit, Donald Flannigan, and after she checked her computer she told me, with a somewhat holy look of disapproval, that I would have to wait for an escort. I sat down and waited for about five minutes, during which time I witnessed several families depart — some obviously distraught, others full of cheer, though manufactured or real, I couldn't tell. A delivery man arrived with three boxes of long-stemmed flowers and a potted poinsettia done up with a red bow. He seemed to be a regular and, before leaving, flirted briefly with the nurse behind the reception desk, offering her — unsuccessfully — an unclaimed bouquet of cut flowers in exchange for a date. My stomach was beginning to curl around itself; I looked around the room for something to concentrate on, some evidence of the normal world, but the magazines were all impossibly old, and so I thumbed through a pamphlet from the New York State Mental Health Commission called "Outpatient Treatment Services: Questions and Answers." When I had exhausted that, I got up to read the notices on a bulletin board across from me with a sign that said "Day Room Activities." For Monday, December nineteenth, patients could attend a poetry workshop, a jewelry making class, and a Christmas tree lighting ceremony presided over by an Episcopal minister, a rabbi (how odd!) and a representative of the Governor's Advisory Council on Mental Health. Patients' families, the board said, were encouraged to attend.

The door behind the reception desk buzzed open and a guard called my name. He — mustachioed, uniformed — introduced himself as my security escort and then ran a metal detector over my body. He looked into the tin I had brought and satisfied himself that it contained nothing more than Danish butter cookies. The CDU, he explained, was on the top floor, which was a secured area, and I should not leave his company at any time. He would deliver me to a nurse there and guide me back. If we became separated, I should follow the blue lines to the nearest nurse's station.

We walked together down a long hall, through three more locked doors and up an elevator that required a key to operate. When we disembarked I found myself in a small reception area similar to the one on the first floor, though the floors were uncarpeted, and the nurse who sat behind the steel desk was quite a bit older. Busty and dour-faced, crammed into her white nurse's uniform, she reminded me not a little of my first grade teacher. A Christmas carol floated down from invisible ceiling speakers.

I signed the register. "You'll have to leave those out here," the nurse said, pointing at the tin of cookies. "Mr. Flannigan's condition does not permit him to have an elective diet at the present time."

"They're just butter cookies," I said. I removed the top and showed her. I thought that if she took one for herself she might feel more inclined to let me take them in. "They're Danish. Donny loves them."

"Yes, I know what they are," she said, eyeing the cookies. Then her faced opened and she smiled in a way that won me over. "Listen, it's very nice of you to bring them, it's just that we have rules. If you want, I can see that they get to some of the other patients. I'm sure they would appreciate it."

It was an impossible offer to refuse. I surrendered the cookies and the nurse, whose nametag said she was Doris Blakely, R.N., rose from behind the desk and with a big ring of keys let me into the wards. The hallway was stuffy and gave the feeling of being hermetically sealed. Light, air, sound — everything seemed pumped in, recycled and stale, through vents. The doors on either side were as large and heavy-looking as the doors on crypts. Each had a small window of wire-reinforced glass, put high to prevent casual peeking. As we walked I questioned her about my friend.

"Mr. Flannigan is here for a three stage treatment," she explained. "The first stage is chemical detox, the second behavior modification through medication and therapy, the third a general rehabilitation to reintegrate the patient into society."

"I see," I said, thinking: Whatever that all means.

The nurse unlocked the door to his room and agreed to wait outside. It was a pleasant room, airy and spacious, with the neutral, artless decor of a motel chain: a wall of tall windows beyond which snow was falling, a television on a swivel stand, a couple of mustard-colored vinyl chairs. Donny lay in bed, watching a game show. His face was greasy and hollow looking, as if made of wax paper, and something about his eyes made me think he wasn't watching the TV at all, that he was watching the wall behind it. The light coming through the window made the linen of his bed look grey. He gave no indication he knew I was there.

"Hey Donny," I said.

I might have yelled Boo! the way he jerked. His eyes shot me and narrowed like a cat's. "Get out of here," he said. He turned his face smartly to the far wall, his body not following. I noticed that he was restrained by thick canvas straps that crossed his chest and legs over the sheets.

"If you think I drove all this way to turn right around and go back, you really are crazy," I said. I pulled one of the chairs around and sat next to the bed. It was an awkward arrangement; the bed was unusually high off the ground, and I found myself face to face with the boxspring. I had to crane my neck to see him. "I tried to bring you some butter cookies but they were confiscated. Sorry."

"My parents sent you, didn't they?" he said, half into the pillow. His voice was childlike and very distant. "You're their fucking spy."

"Hardly," I said. I really thought he was pulling my leg. Why wouldn't his parents come themselves? Donny had made some big mistakes, but sick was sick and the healthy could put up with a lot, I believed, when they had to. I found myself shifting uncomfortably in my chair, listening to the game show that rattled out of the television. I heard the words, "Big money."

"I haven't talked to your parents at all. I heard what happened from my mother."

He turned his head and screamed at me, "Spy! Sneak! Stooge!" Then he began to sing. "Whoooo, are you? Who-oo, who-oo?" His eyes were as round and shiny as new quarters, his voice impossibly rich, like a demonic harmony. His chest rose against the straps. "I say, whoo — "

"Jesus, Donny," I said.

"That's my name don't wear it out. Doris!"

Nurse Blakely stuck her head in the door. "What is it, Donny?"

"Get this lunatic out of my room. Get this do-gooding college boy shithead out of my sight before I really get going."

"Your friend Mr. Conklin came a long way to visit you. He cares about what is happening to you."

"Fuck you, you bag of shit. Don't tell me who my friends are."

"It's OK," I told the nurse. "We never were such great friends, I guess."

"I don't even know you!" he spat at me. "Where is my shot?" He reached down under the bed for the strap releases, crude buckles which I saw were positioned cruelly out of his reach. "Goddamnit Doris, it's time for my fucking shot!"

He thrashed about, arching his back in a series of spasms that ballooned in intensity. His movements reminded me of a film I'd seen on natural childbirth: they were otherworldly, huge and full of high panic. If the bed hadn't been bolted down, I'm sure he would have bounced it across the room and down the hall for whatever shot he wanted.

"I want my meth and I want it now!" he screamed. "For Christsakes, Doris, shoot me the fuck up!"

"I think I shouldn't be here," I said, though I wasn't sure whom I was addressing and by then it hardly mattered. As I backed toward the door Nurse Blakely elbowed past me and shoved Donny's shoulders into the mattress with a force that simply amazed me. His thrashing grew more spastic and involuntary; his jaw was clenched and his skin, especially around the neck, had turned a milky blue. I was appalled and embarrassed and so frightened I thought I might be sick. Then my eyes burst free of him and I was out the door. I saw a doctor marching down the hall trailing two fat orderlies. I didn't stop.

At the desk I waited for the nurse. The guard, who had been waiting for me, looked up from his copy of *Time* magazine. A famous actress smiled out from the cover. "Everything OK?" he said.

"Yeah," I said. "Everything is stupendous."

"Glad to hear it." He went back to the magazine. I watched the clock on the wall and drummed my fingers on the desktop.

After five minutes Nurse Blakely came out, fidgeting with the bun of her hair. She seemed a little surprised to find me. "What's going on?" I asked her. "Why did he act that way?"

"Oh, this is one of his better days. His parents won't even come anymore."

I got the feeling Nurse Blakely had about had it with Donny. "No, really, what's going on with him? He seemed totally crazy."

Nurse Blakely searched my face. "Didn't you know?" she asked. "You really didn't, did you. Your friend's a heroin addict. Actually a mixture of heroin and cocaine is what he's used to, though his body misses the heroin more."

"No," I said. "I don't know what I thought, but I didn't think that."

I was standing at the elevator when I felt her hand on my shoulder.

"Listen, I know that was hard for you, but if it's any help, he probably didn't even know who you were. Long term drug abuse produces something a lot like advanced schizophrenia, something called narcotic delusional syndrome. All that stuff he said is just the poison in his mind. It's the poison talking."

"It's not important," I said. "Really, he's just somebody I grew up with. I don't even know why I came here. I haven't seen him for years. It was just the circumstances."

A bell sounded and the elevator doors glided open. "Narcotic delusional syndrome," I repeated. What was that? "He's insane, isn't he."

From behind her desk, Nurse Blakely nodded. "Well, we don't like to use the word, but I guess technically, yes."

The guard took me down and I drove away. A few inches of fresh snow had fallen and the driving was tricky, though I made it okay. Five miles from home I stopped at a coffeeshop near the train station. Everything seemed to be going fine, but when the waitress came over to take my order, I looked at the laminated menu I was holding, then up at her, her pad and pen poised, and could not remember, through the cloying smell of grease and snowed-on wool and the chatter and clanking that floated out from the kitchen, what it was I wanted. At that moment I didn't know anything at all, except that Donny was insane and I wasn't, and that I wished I hadn't gone.

Navigation

When I was nine and Donny was eleven, our parents became friends, and the lines between our households blurred. The unifying forces in their friendship were a rough similarity of ages, the convenience of our houses to one another, the shared responsibility of getting the road plowed, scraped and landscaped, and a mutual taste for food and cocktails — not much to go on, and I suppose I always knew it was doomed from the start, but for a couple of years my parents seemed almost perpetually entertaining or being entertained by

Sandy and Donald Sr. My mother, who had grown up in opulent circumstances in the city, benefited the most; at Sandra Flannigan's urging, she had her mouse-brown hair dyed to a sensuous auburn and took a job running a boutique in the village that sold unusual jewelry and batiked scarves. The dinners she prepared for the Flannigans were lavish and formal; fragrant French stews of beef, pork and bay leaf, racks of lamb alternately marinated and stuffed, exotic vegetable concoctions I found detestable, glorious flaming deserts. What my father found in the Flannigans I'll never know, though I suspect he was more interested in the law than he let on and enjoyed talking to Donald Sr. in the same way a political exile enjoys hearing about his homeland on the news. When they dined together, at our house or theirs, the children were relegated to a table in the kitchen or games of bumper-pool in the basement, while the adults whooped it up upstairs.

The summer I turned twelve our families jointly chartered a boat to sail up the Maine coast to Canada, from Mt. Desert Island to Grand Manan. It was a strange arrangement really, because the Flannigans did not sail;

I suppose to them it was just another style of vacation. The boat was enormous and peculiar: a sixty-three foot schooner designed by its owner, with an ornately carved bowsprit, a canopy bed in the aft cabin (there were four), two full mains and an inexplicable steel hull that sent the compass wandering like a lost child. She was so large that sometimes it hardly seemed like being on a boat at all; though under sail, working a winch with acres of canvas flying overhead, one had the feeling of living in an age before engines, an age of shipwrecks, sea adventures, *Swallows and Amazons*.

Luther, a leather-skinned, bearded man with a glass eye (he claimed to take it out at night, which fascinated me), attended to the practical matters of keeping the boat's unreliable diesel going, the women seemed perpetually handing out sandwiches and napkins, and my father navigated. In the evenings he spread a chart on the galley table and explained where we were going the next day: "Here," he'd say pointing to a particular harbor or island with the point of a pencil, "or here, if the wind is right." They were just names to me, amoebic yellow shapes bordering the

27

white, but I knew that whatever port we selected would be transformed the next afternoon from a name on paper to a hill of houses and shops and a harbor full of boats. Sailing, I saw, was a way of taking an idea, navigating its distance, and in the end, giving it substance and flesh. After supper my father would take me up on deck and hold the monocular of his sextant to my eye. I was supposed to adjust the apparatus until a particular star came into focus; I never could do it, though I tried hard to please him. As I moved the arm of the sextant, a star would flash on the back of my retina and then vanish, impossibly lost in a sky full of stars.

"You have to know it's there," my father said. We were anchored off an island held in public trust for the maintenance of a herd of wild sheep. "If you know it's there, then it's just a matter of finding it." But still, my hand wasn't steady enough.

Once I lied. "Yes, there it is," I said. "I see it."

"You're sure," my father said.

"Yes, yes, I've got it. Absolutely." I took the sextant from my eye and looked at the numbers on the arm. They didn't mean anything to me, though I'd already fallen for my own lie and was convinced they related to the actual fact of where we were, where we were going.

"Give it here." I handed my father the sextant.

"Congratulations," he said, looking up from his chart. "You've put us somewhere in the middle of Vermont."

The fourth day out, on a long run from Seal Harbor to Cutler, things started to go wrong. The wind died, we pulled down the canvas and started the boat's diesel, which began to miss and twice died completely, setting us adrift on a huge, flat sea. Men dashed below, shouted orders, called up for tools. The day was ruled by a sense of constipated emergency, the drama of not moving. Each time the engine revived I had the feeling of a saving miracle. We lolled on the deck, under a scorching sun, fighting back the day's first inklings of seasickness. In the middle of a game of backgammon Donny went below to go to the head and re-emerged a moment later, yelling about a catastrophe. The head, finicky to begin with, had clogged and begun discharging the contents of the holding tank onto the floor of the main cabin. He described a sea of shit.

An awesome stench greeted us below. "Lookee," Luther said, simultaneously eyeing a school of feces slopping against the bulkhead and the LANDSAT station on the adjacent wall. "Brown trout."

While we beat back the overflow with mops and Luther went after the toilet with a monkey wrench, my father descended the ladder into the bilges. The smell of the cabin and the boat's listless rocking were beginning to sicken me; I looked at Martha, who was rinsing off her mop into a fouled bucket, and saw she was just as green as I felt. My sister and Donny had already fled topside.

We limped into Cutler at sunset. Everyone except my father and Luther was desperately seasick, and after halfheartedly picking at a salad my mother assembled for dinner, the children were put to bed. Donny and I slept in the main cabin in two stacked sideberths, cut into the bulkhead, with curtains that drew for privacy. The smell of shit lingered and I couldn't sleep. There was a porthole next to my head, and through it I heard our parents talking up on deck. The gravity of their tone, and the fact that they seemed to be conducting a secret meeting, told me something was not right.

"What's going on?" I whispered to Donny, to find out if he was asleep.

"Willya shut up?" he said. "I think your father found something in the bilges."

I tried to eke out snatches of the conversation, but my parents' voices seemed to float away from me, just out of reach of the porthole, leaving me with only garbled bits. Mention was made of the Virgin Islands, where Luther's boat was registered, of the Coast Guard, of our destination, Grand Manan, the easternmost island of the Canadian Maritimes. Mostly I heard my father's voice, low and serious, but after a while I heard more and more of the Flannigans until I was certain they were arguing with my father.

I don't know how my father knew I was listening, but he did. The conversation abruptly stopped and then his voice shot me from somewhere close by. "Jake, go to sleep."

I stuck my head out of the porthole and there was his, looking down at me, the perfect black shape of my father's head, silhouetted against the bluish night sky. I could feel the warm air rising off the water, three feet below the back of my head. "Sorry, sir."

"Just go to sleep."

I tried to whisper the next thing I said to him. "What's going on?"

"It's none of your concern," he said, telling me I was inching toward the line. "You have your orders."

My father woke me up early the next morning. "Get your things together," he said.

"What things?" I thought he meant things to go ashore, or the fishing gear.

"Everything. Don't argue, just go. I want you topside in five."

I rolled out of my bunk and stumbled over my parents' packed duffel. My mother stood in the galley, loading food and liquor into boxes. I saw she was trembling; her eyes were red and swollen. "What's going on?" I said.

She didn't look at me. "We're leaving."

"Leaving? We only just got here."

An unopened bottle of gin found its way into a carton of similar bottles. "Your father says we have to leave."

"That's crazy." I tried to wedge myself between my mother and the counter so she would talk to me. "Will you stop doing that and tell me what's going on?"

Half asleep, I didn't see it coming: my mother's open hand, shooting up from her side to slap me squarely on the cheek. It was not a hard blow, but powerful in its symbolic properties — she had never hit me that way before, as a woman hits a man. Her lips set in a prim line, her cheeks delicately puffed with anger, she gave me a look that was unequivocal: if I opened my mouth again, she would hit me again.

In the cabin I dressed quickly, flung my bag up the hatch and clambered topside. My father had drawn the Zodiac alongside and, standing amidships, was loading boxes and duffels from a pile by the open safety line; Lucy was already aboard, hugging herself on the aft bench and looking baffled or just asleep. The sun was just peeking through a stand of pines on the harbor's rocky inlet, darkening them to black and defining the shapes of the waves. It was the same view I had seen the night before, only with the sun reversed, and it gave me the dreamy feeling of *déjà vu*. On the distant blue-grey plain of the open sea I saw the low-slung shapes of trawlers and lobster boats, perhaps a dozen altogether, churning out toward deep water, dragging a wheeling cloud of gulls. Only then did I understand that it was five A.M. at the latest, and everyone else on the boat was asleep — that we were sneaking away.

My father waved at me. "Jake, give me a hand."

By the time we had loaded all our clothes and my father's navigation gear, the Zodiac's tubes were riding dangerously low in the water. "Leave the booze," my father called to my mother, who was standing on the deck holding the box over the safety line. She looked like a Russian peasant girl standing there in her red windbreaker, her hair done up in a matching red bandana. "Goddamnit, just leave it there, Suze."

"I will *not* leave without this," my mother said. "We paid for it and we're taking it with us."

"We paid for the boat too," he said, adjusting the choke on the Zodiac's outboard. "We're leaving it."

The carton of liquor pulled to her chest, my mother gave made no sign of giving in. "Oh, for Petesakes," my father said. "Jake, go up and help your mother."

I stiff-armed myself to the deck and took the box from her arms. She let it go, though for an instant I had thought she might fight me for it, and I didn't know what I would do, what I *should* do, if that happened. I just didn't have enough information, and my sense of loyalty, so expertly directed in the past, was totally confounded by the prospect of mortifying her on behalf of the same emergency for which she had previously struck me across the face. But she didn't fight me. I put the box on the deck by the open hatch and, taking her hand, balanced her weight — so light she was! — as she maneuvered herself into the bobbing Zodiac.

My father was still fiddling with the choke switch. "Do you need me right away?" I called down.

"What?" He didn't look up. "Get down here."

"I'll be right there," I said, backing down the hatch. "I have something to do."

I knew I only had a minute before my father sent my sister after me and I caught hell, but still I lingered for a moment in the cabin, filled with the incipient nostalgia of one abandoning ship. The cabinets in the galley stood open, their doors floating on their hinges in time to the shiftings of the boat's massive steel keel. Red lights raced across a diode display on the ship's radio panel, searching for signals. In the magnifying acoustics of the cabin, I could discern the creaking of the hull, the lapping of waves against it, even, for an instant, the sound of the bottom of the sea: *Hurry, hurry.*

I pulled back Donny's curtain and shook him on the shoulder. "Donny, we're going."

"What?" He rolled over and jerked awake. "Where are we going?"

"Not you, me," I said. "My father says we have to leave."

He rubbed the sleep from his eyes, looked out the porthole, then back at me. "I don't get it," he said.

"I don't get it either." I heard my father calling, and then the sound of the Zodiac's engine catching and driving seawater through its impellers; it reached me first as a high pitched wail, quickly underscored by a lagging, tremulous roar; the engine's aural components separated by the metal bulkhead as if strained through a filter. The feeling of saying goodbye to Donny was like that, too: part of me, the part saying goodbye, was ahead of the rest. Not knowing what else to do, I grabbed Donny's hand and shook it. "This has nothing to do with us," I said. "Just remember that. I'll see you in Redding."

When I got back topside, the Zodiac was still there, and my father helped me down. The schooner had fallen a hundred yards away before he spoke. We were sitting next to one another in the stern. "When I ask you to do something at sea, you just do it."

"I'm sorry," I explained, "but I don't want to talk about it." It was the first time I had said anything like that to my father. A rental car took us from Cutler to Bangor, six hours away, where we waited in the airport snack bar for our flight to Boston, changing for LaGuardia. Outside the open windows, small turbo-props and six-seater Cessnas taxied, hurling hot air and the smell of tar back into the terminal. The kitchen was out of most everything — a tour group had just come through at the lunch hour and cleaned the place out, the waitress said — so we ordered a pitcher of iced tea and egg salad sandwiches all around. I was ravenous and wolfed down three.

After the waitress had cleared our plates my father said, "I suppose you kids would like to know what happened."

Lucy, who had retreated into a mood, shrugged and said she was tired of the trip anyway and wanted to go home. All summer she had been saying things like that, disassociating herself from the family and retreating into her books like the prima donna I thought she was. She infuriated me, and as far as I was concerned, waving off my father made her not just a prima donna but also an idiot. I was just about to say something on the subject when my father spoke again.

"Yesterday I went down into the bilges and found some things that disturbed me, disturbed me very much."

Suddenly, I knew. Not just what they had been talking about the night before, but the subject of other whispered conversations and funny, sidelong glances I realized had been exchanged since we'd picked up the boat in Southwest Harbor. "It's drugs," I said. "Luther was running drugs into Canada."

My sister punched my leg. "Quiet, Jake."

"That," my father said, "is the general gist of it."

"We're just sorry we endangered you kids," my mother said. There was something sad and defeated in her voice, a sense of shame from which there was no turning back. Her eyes had misted over again, which I knew would annoy my father. "You have to know that we had no idea."

The knowledge that I awakened that morning aboard a vessel carrying illicit cargo filled me, top to bottom, with a voluptuous, moral thrill. "How do you know?" I asked my father. "Did you see it?"

"Don't badger your father," my mother said.

"I want to know what he saw."

"I don't have to explain any more than I already have," my father said. The waitress arrived with bowls of vanilla ice cream I didn't recall anyone ordering. "Eat your dessert."

I never knew for certain whether or not Luther was running drugs, or what, precisely, my father had seen: bales of pot stacked like hay, white powder in jars (what did drugs look like? I wasn't sure) or just some suspicious-looking compartments that, in his mind, combined with the boat's bizarre hull, Caribbean registry and Luther's itinerant lifestyle, and added up to the general gist of drugs. We never spoke of it again, not in so many words. The Flannigans stayed aboard, the boat reached Canadian waters the next day, and as far as I know, nothing at all happened. They had a fine vacation, a little angered by our absence I suppose, but in the end enjoyed themselves so much that they chartered Luther's boat in the Caribbean that winter with a couple from the city. My parents heard through friends, and I through my parents, that Mr. Flannigan, drunk as a lord, had done a swandive off the bosun's chair and sprained his neck — further proof that they were not our kind of people, that they were a reckless, immoral and forgettable episode.

Poison

As it turned out, I never did become much of a ball player. A new history teacher at my school introduced us to lacrosse, and within a year its exotic equipment and licensed violence had won the hearts of all the boys and supplanted baseball entirely. For a while I gave this new game a try, though I wasn't suited to it. I was timid about getting hit, my cheap gloves made it difficult to maneuver the stick, I couldn't run with a cup on, and so I spent most of my time on the bench, bored to distraction. Before long my relegation to the bench came so routinely I would go straight there at the beginning of scrimmage and mentally decline irregular Latin verbs, my head boiling in the helmet. I thought myself so worthless to the team that in the spring of my ninth grade year I cut a game to finish an English paper and was tossed off the team. In hindsight, I suppose cutting a lacrosse game to write an English paper was a veiled choice of some kind, and I felt rather adult about it at the time, though my coach didn't share my opinion. As he saw it, I was a lazy, treasonous disgrace (they'd lost the game, though I doubted I could have helped) and in front of my mother, a gathered crowd of peers and three teachers whose respect I wanted to keep and somehow did, he chewed me out in the school parking lot and exiled me forever to a gulag of papers and books.

Donny didn't become much of a ball player, either. I didn't see him much anymore. His parents stopped coming out, and when they did, my parents pretended not to notice, as if by prior agreement. They tolerated my lingering friendship with Donny in the same way they tolerated my tastes in music, clothing and food, which by then were hopelessly teenaged. In the first spring of my banishment from organized athletics, I went into the city to stay with him and take in a twilight double-header at Shea, a spectacle I still enjoyed, though I'd long since lost track of the players and their statistics and was more interested in the prospect of Mr. Flannigan buying us beer, which he loved to do. I had never been to the Flannigans' New York apartment before, didn't know my way around New York, and so I asked Donny to meet me at Grand Central under the big clock.

I arrived on time, a little after five. Rush hour was in full swing. I positioned myself with my back to the wall beneath the *Newsweek* clock, watching the booming mob for Donny to appear. Men and women hurried by with briefcases and umbrellas, checked their watches as they raced to the platforms. The bar on the upper deck was crowded and loud. It seemed impossible that, in this mayhem, two people could successfully find one another. A half-hour passed, and thinking I might have made a mistake (had we said the clock? Perhaps it was giant Kodak advertisement, or the information gazebo), I set out across the floor. At one of the big newsstands I was buying a *Sports*

Illustrated and a chocolate bar when my hand groped at nothing in my back pocket and I realized my wallet was gone.

It was sometime later, standing under that great white-faced clock after a useless conversation with a policeman, that Martha stepped out of the crowd and walked toward me. She was dressed in her school uniform — tartan kilt, white blouse, navy kneesocks and loafers — and toted a heavy-looking leather bookbag over her shoulder. I hadn't expected to see her, and I hugged her desperately. "Where's Donny?" I asked, my arms around her. "Oh, Martha, I was robbed."

She looked at me blankly. "What did you say?"

"Robbed," I said. "They got my money, my ticket, everything." I related what had happened, though my story didn't sound anywhere near as heroic as I would have liked. Short of telling out-right fiction, I couldn't make myself out to be anything other than a victim and a rube.

"You shouldn't have kept it in your back pocket," she said when I was done.

"I don't even have enough money to take the train back. What's the matter with Donny?"

Martha looked suddenly off toward the Great Hall. For a moment I thought she was looking for Donny. "He's just sick is all," she said, and her voice, which seemed to tiptoe, told me she was lying. "He told me to tell you the game was off."

I had forgotten all about the game. Her mention of it seemed strangely irrelevant, as quaint and dated as a year-old newspaper. It sort of made me angry. "What do you mean just sick," I said. "What is that?"

Martha sighed. "Look, it's more complicated than that. You'll just have to go back."

"Martha, I can't go back. See this?" I took out my change and showed it to her. It felt like nothing in my hand; it felt like being broke. "This is all I have left. A dollar and twenty-two cents."

"You could call you parents. Couldn't they send you a ticket, or something?"

"I don't want to call my parents. I want you to tell me what's wrong with Donny." Martha fidgeted with the pleats of her tartan skirt, hiked up the book bag that hung from her shoulder. I knew she was about to tell me. "Oh God, I'm not going to lie about this one. I suppose you're going to find out soon enough anyway. Donny got kicked out of St. Francis."

I was flabbergasted. Kicked out — it was beyond imagining, an utter catastrophe. "I don't believe it."

"He was smoking pot in the bathroom with three other boys. The dean of students caught them."

"You're lying," I said. "Tell me you're lying."

Martha frowned, her cheek bunching like a baby's fist around the scar at the corner of her mouth. As long as I had known her, that scar had acted as the center of her emotional gravity. Right then it was telling me that Donny had got precisely what he deserved. "It was the middle of the day," she said acidly. "Of course my stupid brother got caught."

There was nothing to do then but go see him. We exited the station, got ourselves turned around, and ended up scaling Manhattan island by Fifth Avenue, past the unreal greenness of the park, the cathedral, the big stores. Behind their windows, mannequins struck harsh poses against backdrops of black velvet, the air was thick as steam, the sound of car horns was like a smothering cloth over everything. Somewhere in the Sixties we caught a crosstown bus — the operator drove with a wild determination, spinning the wheel this way and that, bravely navigating intersections jammed with delivery vans and tank-like Checker cabs — changing at Third to continue our ascent. All the while I was thinking about Donny, what terrible things would happen to him after this black day, how he had ruined his life.

The Flannigans lived in an older apartment between Eightieth and Eighty-first, overlooking the East River. We got off at Third and Eightieth and walked the rest of the way. By the time we arrived, sweat had soaked my shirt and I was breathing hard, though dusk had fallen and a cool breeze blew off the river. The building was built of grey, soot-stained stones and, gave the appearance of a monolith. Martha and I rode up in the old fashioned elevator. As the floors floated past I suddenly remembered Donny's parents.

"They're in Chicago," Martha told me. "They haven't even heard yet."

"Your dad was supposed to take us to a ball game."

"How do I know?" Martha said, unlocking their door. "A friend of theirs died or something. They left this morning."

The Flannigans' apartment was an elegant affair, unlike any home I had seen before. Martha led me through the marble-floored hallway, the big steel kitchen, a gigantic, flowing living room with mirrors on one wall and windows overlooking the river on the other. There was art on the walls, there were busts on pedestals, there was a television in the den the size of a home-movie screen. Beams of light, vaguely metallic in color, shot the walls from tracks on the ceiling and made me think of museums I'd been to. The top of the dining room table was glass, an arrangement I had never seen before, and I wondered how one ate, looking at everyone's feet.

We reached Donny's room. The door was closed, but through it, I heard the thump of music, turned up loud.

"You're not going to like this," Martha said, and walked away.

Somehow it didn't seem right or necessary to knock, and I let myself in. The shades were drawn, and I stood by the door for a moment and let my eyes adjust. I discerned a bed, a dresser. Strewn clothes materialized, shelves of books and trophies, posters tacked at odd angles on the walls. Nothing about it matched the rest of the apartment, and I got the feeling Donny's parents didn't come in there very often.

Donny sat on the floor, his back wedged against a small couch; he was fantastically stoned.

I knelt in front of him. "Why are you doing this?" I said. "Why is this happening?"

Donny's eyes landed on me and rolled away. "Look who's here," he said. A limp hand waved me off. "The Latin scholar."

I was furious; not so much at him, but at the rate things seemed to be happening, the velocity of my life. I felt as if I were taking a test designed for me to fail. I yanked him by the shirt collar and pulled his face within a foot of mine. His breath wafted over me, sweet and smokey; his eyes were bloated with red vessels. I couldn't find my reflection anywhere in them.

"Oh, forget it," I said. I released him and sat down in a black leather armchair.

"That's right, just forget it." His hand fumbled in the breast pocket of his jacket and brought out a half-full zip-lock bag and a small wooden pipe with a bronze bowl shaped like an upturned thimble. A marijuana leaf was etched in the metal.

"How can you waste yourself this way?" I asked, watching him pack it. "You're too talented for this." Instantly, I regretted saying it; they were not my words. When had I grown up to become my father?

Donny scowled. "What would you know about it? Do you have any idea what it is like to be me?"

"Don't be an idiot. Of course I do."

"Yeah, it's pretty fucking great, being me."

For a while we just sat there, looking at each other in the bad light. In a sad way, I felt as if I were all alone in the room. I was remembering things that happened, years ago. Things we did.

"I've always looked up to you, you know. My wallet was stolen at the station, and all I thought was: Donny will help me, Donny will know what to do."

"Oh," he said, rolling his head, "cut the shit. Please cut that shit out."

"Are you listening? I said my wallet was stolen at the station. I'm telling you I was robbed, and I wanted you there. You told me you would be there."

"Poor baby. Lost his wallet. Want some advice? Keep it in your front pocket."

He lit the bowl and sucked on the end of the stem, pulling the burning embers into a glowing coal. The shadows it cast upward onto his face were dark and strange. Watching him smoke, I filled up with the image of it.

"What does it do to you?"

He laughed absurdly, jetting smoke. "It makes me stoned."

"No, I mean does it make you feel better, or smarter, or what?" I leaned forward in the chair. I wanted to be understood. "Do you know things you didn't know before?"

He tapped the ashes into an ashtray and reloaded the bowl, and I thought for a second he'd lost the thread of the conversation. The air around me was pungently sweet, as if handfuls of rich spices — clove, saffron, powdered sugars — had been tossed into the air. It reminded me of my mother's cooking, and saliva washed down the walls of my mouth.

"Nah," he said, looking around at the dark nothing of his bedroom. He handed me the pipe backward, as if he were handing me a knife. I took the stem in my hand and peered into the bowl. I felt the rising heat bore into my forehead, the smoke teasing my nostrils, singing my eyelashes. It was like waiting for a pitch. I closed my eyes. I swear, as my lips touched the wood of the stem, I felt myself turning inside out.

"You'll see," Donny said. "It just makes you stoned."

Martha

The summer Martha turned fourteen, she went into the hospital for the last operation on her scar, and it was botched. Her parents brought her home to Redding one bright day in late June. Donny and I were waiting in the driveway, tossing pebbles at the trees. Half her face was bandaged, and her legs, laid across the leather of the Jag's back seat, had been wrapped with a tartan blanket. The image was grandmotherly and had a certain heroic quality of doom and hopelessness. Donny and I had split a fat joint in the woods and were about as wasted as two boys could get and still help an injured girl up to her bed without laughing.

Oh, there was lots of encouraging talk. "Operations of this kind," Mr. Flannigan said, "take time to work themselves out." Or, as Mrs. Flannigan put it, "Let's not think about it until the bandages come off." There was just enough talk to know that the surgeon had said something and it was botched. We were a conspiracy of false hope.

Part of Martha's lip had been grafted, and she had to eat through a straw, like a prize-fighter whose jaw had been wired shut. Donny and I brought milkshakes to her bedroom on trays. As her stitches dissolved she graduated to scrambled eggs, pudding, cottage cheese, small episodes of speech. What, behind the wordlessness of her bandages, that brave, inward stare, was she thinking? She was thinking: I will be the scarred version of myself the rest of my days. I will look how I look. There seemed no kidding Martha on that score. She went into New York a week later to have the bandages removed, and came back with a fresh dressing, which wasn't part of the

original blueprint. The implication was ob-
vious.

"I can't look at her," Donny told me. Martha had just come home the second time.
We were hanging around the kitchen, waiting for his parents to leave so we could get
high. The plan that summer was to dupe
our parents by diluting their sense of our
right selves with broader and more fre-
quent episodes of boosted incoherence.
Which is to say, we stayed stoned by staying
stoned.

Being straight made me bored and
cranky. The day was hot and seemed to
crawl. I fiddled with a salt shaker that
Donny and I were sliding at each other
across the table like a puck. "What's not to
look at? They're just bandages."

"It's the idea of the bandages."

"You smoke too much," I said. "They are
what they are."

Mrs. Flannigan strode into the kitchen.
She wore a wrap-around golf skirt and silk
blouse, and the purse that hung from the
curve of her elbow had little green whales
embroidered on it. Her lipstick was that
shade of red I had come to associate with
pushy women. I was at the Flannigans'

house so much that summer that she sometimes said motherly things to me.

"Your father and I," she said to both of
us, "are going out now."

"Fine," Donny said sourly.

"There's steak from last night for your
lunch, and soup for Martha."

"We'll give it to her." Mrs. Flannigan came
around the table and cupped the back of
Donny's head with her hand, mussing his
hair a little. "It's going to be fine," she said.

"I was just saying that," I said.

"Why so sad, baby?" Donny's head
seemed to shrink from her, his eyes nar-
rowing on the the salt shaker he was spinning with the tip of his finger. Mrs.
Flannigan bent at the waist and put her face
close to Donny's cheek. "Baby, why so sad?"

"I'm not sad," Donny said. "We'll fix her
the soup."

"Make it chicken," Mrs. Flannigan said.
"OK, baby? I think she's tired of everything
else."

Donny and I watched them go from an
upstairs window. His bedroom, tucked
under the eaves of the old farmhouse, was
decorated in the style of a desert brothel.
We had made a project of it at the start of
the summer: hanging tapestries to fall like

the walls of a tent, swapping the chairs for old mattresses from the attic. We cranked open a window, got the fan going and sat down on the pillows to smoke the pot Donny kept in an old army lock-box, loading the bowl of the tall glass bong he kept behind a loose board in his closet. We had named the bong "Benny" so that we might refer to him obliquely among mixed company. Together we had gone in on a lid which Donny bought from someone he knew in the city, someone from his new school, which I gathered was quite a place. They had a lounge with cots in it so students could lie down between classes. We still didn't know where to buy pot in Redding.

We smoked for a time, sinking into the mattresses, letting the shadow of the whirling fan blade suggest all manner of things to us. So, I don't know who it was exactly that stirred the pot into Martha's soup; but I know no one objected. The leaves gathered broth and grease, floating darkly like bits of some seasoning. We added some Parmesan cheese. We took it up to her on the usual tray, feeling excited and happy and good about what we were doing.

Martha lay on top of the sheets in sweats, penciling-in a crossword from a book of puzzles. A second pencil was locked in the unbandaged corner of her mouth. It looked like an arrow she had snatched from the air with her teeth, and for a second, I thought she had done such a thing and was amazed. I was very wasted and receptive to visual suggestion.

"Lunch time," Donny sang. He carried the tray over to her on the tips of his fingers and deposited it on her lap with a waiterly flourish. He had always been graceful in just that way. "Soup du jour."

"Du Donny," I said.

"Du Jake," he added, putting his big hand on my shoulder as I thought an older brother might do. Martha thanked us and maneuvered herself to a more workable position from which to eat soup. I looked at the clean white square of her bandage and at her eyes; and suddenly I realized that we had dosed her soup with enough dope to keep her up for a week, that I could lurch away from myself only so far; that I just couldn't do it.

"That doesn't look right," I said.

Martha looked up, the spoon balanced sweetly in her hand. "Wha'?"

I gestured to the tray on her knees. I counseled myself to appear as if I had just discovered something. "Your soup. There was a dent in the can, and it doesn't look right to me." I sniffed at the bowl and then lifted the tray from her lap. I didn't want to get too close because I had spilled some rancid water from the bong on my jeans and I thought she would smell it. "No, definitely, not right. We'll get you some more."

I thought we were about to get away clean; was practically out the door when Martha said, "What's in the soup, Donny?" The way she said it, it sounded like, 'Was inna shoop, Donny.'

"There's nothing in the soup," he said.

"We'll get you some more," I said, going out. "I'll just be a minute."

I was opening another can when Donny burst into the kitchen. I had poured the other stuff down the drain, glad to see it go.

"Fuck you," he said. His breathing came fitfully, as if he had run through all the rooms of the house. I didn't say anything. "Just fuck you. Let me do that."

"I'm making her some fresh soup."

"This isn't your house and if anyone is going to make soup it's going to be me.

Why are you even here? I don't know why you're here."

"We had no right to do that," I said. "That was cruel." I poured the soup into a clean pan and lit the burner. It made a pleasing, kitcheny whump sound. I stirred the soup, Donny's eyes on me. I could feel them, hard as ice pellets, poking the back of my head; could smell his hair and the pot on his breath, sweet and smokey like an old woman's room, mingling with the icy lick of the burner gas. How could people not know we smoked as much as we did?

"It was your idea as much as mine."

"I don't care whose idea it was," I said.

Donny whirled around the kitchen, shoving and hitting things, tipping over an empty coatrack that crashed to the floor, and then returned to the spot just behind me. I refused to look at him. "Why are you even here?" he said.

The soup began to bubble. I thought Donny might hit me, or do something to the soup. If he wanted to hit me that was OK. I stood before the stove, blocking his passage to it, stirring the clear, untampered broth with a wooden spoon. The pot we had smoked still whirred inside my head, but through its effects I had the vague sense of doing something noble, that I was almost clean again, and getting hit by Donny might be part of that. That's what I was thinking when suddenly his eyes weren't there anymore, and I turned around: I was alone in the Flannigans' kitchen.

I made a big production of the second lunch tray. When the soup was ready I rummaged through the Flannigans' cupboards and found crackers and arranged them in a fan on a small plate. The first tray still lay on the counter and I didn't even like looking at it; I fetched another from the pantry, and covered it with a white linen placemat. I discovered, searching for something to make the tray complete, three small glass vases on top of the refrigerator; I ran some tapwater into one and then went out to the Flannigans' yard and picked a rose from the sun-drenched vines that curled around the dog run fence. Then I took Martha her real lunch.

Martha was sitting on her bed, just as she had been when we left, her bandaged face turned toward the window. The shadow of the window's cross-beam fell across her bandaged cheek and her eyes appeared in full light, framed by the dark band and glowing wisps of her blonde hair. At that moment, I could not have said how old either one of us was.

"Hi again." I entered and put the tray on her bedside table, nudging aside a pile of magazines and puzzle books. I backed away and watched Martha watch her lunch. Steam and the briny smell of soup wafted from the bowl. From the table, the rose bent toward her like lips reaching to kiss the head of a child.

"I checked the can. I thought this looked OK."

"Mmmm," Martha said, nodding slightly. "'kay."

We looked at each other for a long moment, and finally I said, "I don't know why we did that." I put my hands on my head in the soft light of the bedroom, and when I closed my eyes my center of gravity shot up like a bird through the top of my head and it was all I could do to brace my shoulder against the frame of the door and pry my eyes open to rebind myself to the face of this earth. The miracle of getting upstairs with the second tray intact — soup, linen, rose — overwhelmed me. "Oh, we're really messed up," I said.

"S'okay," Martha said. "C'mere."

I sat on the foot of her bed, and then I was crying. All I could think about was what we had almost done, the confusion of it, the pollution. I buried my face in the swirled linens of the bed, which smelled like Martha and warm bedclothes and the air of the Flannigans' house. I could feel the hard bone of her thigh against my temple, and then her leg shifted and my head nestled in a shallow valley of muscle and her hand was on my head; the scarred girl's hand was on my head, and I wept until I was asleep, and that was the first time I slept in bed with a girl.

Seamus

When I was twenty-eight, my wife Kathy and I had a son, whom we named Seamus, after my father. We were living in New York, where I made my living as a journalist for one of the wire services, and Kathy packaged mortgages for a large commercial bank. Seamus was an accident of statistics but one which we agreed was happy. It would help us establish our priorities, we said, move us into new stages, teach us things that could not be learned in any other way.

During the early months Kathy was cranky, gluttonous and threw up her coffee and juice every day at precisely seven-thirty. Then her body found its rhythm and we went shopping. We bought baby clothes, baby furniture, assorted baby paraphernalia, books called "What To Name the Baby." We searched, without success, for an affordable two bedroom apartment on the Upper West Side. Kathy is a beautiful woman in my eyes — I have never seen a woman who looked better to me — and at night I watched her undress and admired the changes in her body as one might admire the second and third versions of a novel more than the first. On a low stool at the end of the claw-footed tub I washed her hair and back and as her breasts and belly swelled I thought: this is it, this is life, this is why we believe ourselves to be blessed.

Kathy's bank was accommodating on the subject of pregnancy leave. She made more money than I did — a lot more — so we agreed a year off on her part was all we could afford. Then I would take a year and finish a book I had been fooling with and look after the baby. This was a complicated arrangement, but we felt we had the presence of mind, the unselfishness, to make it work. And as it turned out, we surprised everyone and pulled it off.

Kathy's water broke three weeks early, while I was in Rome covering a Bishops' Synod for the month of October. I think the Service gave me the assignment because I spoke Italian and they were thinking of moving me permanently to Rome on that basis. Kathy's time was near, and a move to Italy would have caused all sorts of problems, but it was a juicy assignment and so I agreed, somewhat reluctantly, to go. The day our son was born I was in the wire offices on Via Pandolfini when a telegram arrived: "My water just broke in the middle of a client meeting. Stop. Yuck. Stop. Puddle highly frowned upon, will probably lose job. Stop. Have no money for cab so will crawl to hospital. Stop. Whatever you're doing, stop. Stop. Love, Kathy." Something extraordinary happened to me when I read those words: I multiplied. I tipped the delivery boy thirty-thousand lire (all I could find in the petty cash drawer), ran down to the airline office and charged a ticket on Alitalia, rode to DaVinci airport in a barrelling Roman cab, and was seated in the cavernous belly of a nearly-empty 747 bound for New York without missing so much as a beat from office to air. I tried watching the movie, writing about my feelings, sleeping, but could find no purchase in any of these, so I ended up drinking five little bottles of Vodka and swapping stories about pregnancy, birth and other occasions for inspired madcappery with the flight crew the whole way to New York, which rose like a turreted castle from the fog-choked sea shortly after dawn.

It was a little before 7:00 A.M. when I got to the hospital. In the hallway, an unshaven Indian doctor told me, somewhat gravely, that the baby had been delivered by Caesarean — we had anticipated that possibility, had we not? yes, we had — but mother and child were fine. Then he took me to her. Kathy looked like she'd been through a war. Her face was ashen and damp and her hands rested lightly on the sheets covering her belly, as if she could not believe she had shrunk so. When I hugged her she started to cry, but when I suggested we name our son MacDuff the quality of her crying changed and eventually she started to laugh. Neither of us knew, at that time, if she'd be able to have another.

Half-drunk on jet lag I flagged down a nurse in the hall and asked, with the theatrical rudeness of a new father, to have our son brought up. He was small, I admitted, but healthy and capable of travel, which I told the nurse I knew something about. I suppose the nurse thought me a complete lunatic, but she said she'd make the necessary inquiries and went away. After a few minutes the door to Kathy's room opened and the same nurse backed in with a blue bundle in her arms. God, I thought without yet seeing our boy, God he is beautiful, look what God hath wrought. I am not a religious man — at least, not formally — but I experienced the same unembarrassed awe in the presence of the nurse's sky-blue bundle as I had in Saint Peter's Basilica, where sunbeams fall in perfect, smoky shafts from the high windows in the cupola to give the impression that God exists, pays attention, and takes the form of light. The nurse placed him gingerly in the crook of Kathy's elbow, and tears poured from my eyes. Half a day before I had been in Rome and now I was in New York looking at my son, cradled in the arms of my beautiful wife, a conspiracy of fortune that seemed, to me, miraculous. Our boy was tiny and hairless. His skin, bluish and veined, appeared to glow with an inner illumination, like stained glass. In his face, an old man's face, I saw the shape of centuries in his making. I could not believe how in love I was.

I leaned forward, put out my finger for him to take. Blind, he seized it and pulled it toward his mouth. I was surprised by the hard tips of his nails, opaque as seaglass. His grip on my finger was instinctual and firm. "Bat," I said, not knowing why. "Hey slugger: *bat, ball.*"

Farewell

The summer Martha turned fifteen and her operation was botched, neither one of us had ever kissed anybody, and it seemed the thing to do to kiss each other. So the summer of getting high became the summer of Martha, and as July faded into August and Martha's bandages came off — the scar was still there, though diminished, and the skin of her cheek had an evener tone — we went out to movies and dances at her parents' country club and moved by increments to the moment when our lips would meet and we would begin exploring the world in new ways. It was a biological thing between us but it had its implied, contractual aspect; for we had known each other longer than we had known any other boy or girl. It was as if the world had been created for us to kiss in.

We realized we would kiss each other on a Sunday morning, a week before it happened. My father had taken us out sailing on his boat, but there was no wind, so we went in early. He left us at the pier to unrig and went in to have a beer at the bar in the small clubhouse. There wasn't much to un-rigging a catboat, and Martha and I were sitting on the edge of the dock, talking and watching the boats, when suddenly the conversation evaporated without a trace and we were looking right at one another, wondering where it had run off to. The moment felt frozen, and there was a powerful sense of something bound to happen, of frantic activity in the midst of nothing, like a swarm of bees over our heads.

"What are you doing?" Martha said, and her cheeks blushed, which I had never seen them do. Waves lapped at the pylons and the hulls of dinghies, a water-skier shot past with a whoop. Martha wore a green bikini top, and beneath the line of green her stomach was flat and tan; our bare elbows were touching, and through them an erotic current passed that numbed my feet.

I said, "I'm not doing anything, what are you doing?" and I nudged her shoulder with mine and we laughed, recovering ourselves. I was very embarrassed and very, very happy. When my father came down, his lips wet with beer, he called me "Smiley," which he hadn't done in years; so, I guessed it must have showed.

I finally kissed her the next Sunday when it looked like time was running out. I was going away to school in a week. Lucy was already gone, Donny was, where? — I didn't know. Most of the time he stayed in the city with his father, who came out on the weekends. I walked over to the Flannigans' at night, and Martha came out onto the porch and sat down with me on the iron-rod couch. I thought: here goes. I put my arm around her and our noses brushed past one another like cars in opposite lanes of traffic and while each was trying to look back at the other's passing nose our lips sustained a tiny, head-on collision.

Martha's lips were closed and a little dry. The scar at the corner of her mouth felt like a staple had been put there, but otherwise, kissing felt fine to me, better than fine and also a little strange. But, it was not at all disgusting. It was warmer than I had dared imagine, and there was a saltiness and a meaty flavor, and it seemed I could never quite make myself as aware of events as I wanted to be. The whole thing seemed slightly robotic. But then Martha's lips parted, her breath filling my mouth, and I experienced the biggest, most pleading erection of my life, and I had had some doozies. My center of gravity shifted closer to hers and I imagined myself passing through her like a ghost. I moved my hand between the buttons of her sweater and was fumbling with them and hoping she might help me, when a titanic force vaulted me to my feet and hurled me against the anterior wall of the house. For a second I thought I had been hit by a car, or a tornado, or simply lifted by God. It was Donny.

"You sonuvabitch," he spat.

"What the hell," I said, knowing I was finally going to be hit. I tried to put my hands in front of my face, but too late; the flat plane of his fist was already rushing up at me and caught me squarely in the side of the head. It made a sound like a ball in a glove and unscrewed my eyes so that, in a flash, the room divided like a cell and I saw two: two iron-rod couches, two glowing Chinese lanterns, two Donnys and two Marthas. As I fell to the floor Martha bounced to her feet. Donny kicked at me, and dimly I felt where the rubber of his sneaker had burned my arm. I rolled and another blow hit me straight in the cushion of my ass. Martha screamed and pounded his back.

"You leave him alone!"

Then he left and came back with a baseball bat which I surmised, by the way he carried it, he planned to use on my head. I think he might have killed me. But the first punch had worn off, I was on my feet, and I always had been faster than Donny. Something about his anger, his sloppy, lunatic's wrath, struck me as slapsticky and unreal — there was no heft to it, no weight — and as he raged around the porch with a baseball bat huffing and snorting and saying "fuck" I started to laugh with a proud, indestructible giddiness. I didn't think my mind had ever been as clear, my reflexes as rarified. His bat slammed down on the porch railing inches from where I'd just stood, and I was flying over the railing into the yard. I wanted to taunt him, to extend his humiliation as long as I could and orchestrate it with a thousand small defeats. So I shot this way and that, cutting serpent shapes across the lawn. I dashed straight toward him and floated back on the balls of my feet. His bat fanned broad white swaths in the black air.

"Lookout, lookout!" Martha cried.

Lights blinked on in the house, there were footsteps, commotions within. I looked and as I looked Donny gained one step on me and my upper arm received the full, flying force of the bat. The pain was a hot explosion and it reached its fingers across my back and chest and bent me double. I thought: *I am going to die.* Then: *Donny is about to kill someone, he is about to kill me.* I was looking at the grass and thinking that grass was not such a bad thing to be looking at at the moment of one's death, when I realized several seconds had passed and no killing blow had fallen. I forgot about the grass and scrambled for the edge of the woods and shielded myself behind a split-trunk elm just as the bat hit *smack!* on the knotty wood. I grabbed the thick end of it, using the tree as a fulcrum, and held on.

For an instant, our faces were pulled together in the no-man's land between the split trunks. Donny's face was bloated and vague; sweat greased the bangs of his hair into points on his forehead, and his breath washed a rotten smell over me, which after a second I recognized as the smell of confusion. I saw that he had taken something, was riding the crest of some incredible drug, and that in the landscape of his mind he was only protecting his sister from the monsters of his own wobbly dread. Why do some people simply fail to live in the world? Why must some grapple while others walk freely toward the light? I had believed, chased off the porch by a man with a bat, that Donny had just gone bad, or crazy, that Donny was no longer Donny and that pity was wasted on him; but things were never that simple.

I yanked hard on the thick end of the bat and tore it from his fingers. I was surprised, and not surprised, at how easily I did it. Our faces were still only a foot apart. "You don't see what you're doing," I said. "You think you're doing a right thing but you're not."

His father was rushing down the porch steps. His white shirt glowed in the spotlight like a truncated ghost. He was yelling, "Donny, what in the hell!"

"It's OK," I said to him. Then to Donny, "I'm taking this."

"So take it," he said. "It's yours anyway." Then the air wooshed out of him and he sat down on the floor of the woods.

"I don't know what will happen to you," I said.

Donny was covering himself with leaves, scooping them over his legs like a boy playing with sand. "Yes, you do," he said.

"Yes, I do," I said, "but I can't do anything about that now." The Flannigans were coming toward us, their long shadows mingling and filling the lawn. I waved, feeling very much as if I loved them and would never see them again. Then I turned away, and carrying the bat, I jogged across the meadow toward home, and by the time I arrived I could no longer hear their voices, they had dissolved, handsomely, into the trees.

Homer

When I was thirty-two and Donny was thirty-four and Kathy was thirty and Seamus was four and Martha was thirty-one and my sister Lucy was thirty-three and living in Los Angeles with her husband (a bookish documentary film-maker who shot a mean game of eight-ball and was, I don't know how old), my father, retired from the County Board and the Firm, suffered a heart attack out on his new catboat, "Felicity." The thing that hit him was minor as heart attacks go; he managed to sail back to the dock, tie up and unrig before lying down against the gas pump and asking the harbormaster, with a certain grave politeness I'm sure, to summon an ambulance with all the bells and whistles. He recovered quickly, but my father, Yankee to the last, plumbed the depths of his scarred heart for some practical wisdom to be learned and surfaced with the not-surprising axiom that life, in this case his life, was short and should not be squandered. The immediate result was that he wanted to see his grandson and namesake more often and played not a few violins to make it happen.

"Who knows when I'll go," he said over the phone.

"Don't be silly," I said, or Kathy said, if she took the call. "You're going to live a long time, Dad."

He said, "This has taught me a valuable lesson, and the lesson is to take no bullshit from your kids. You can bring my grandson up anytime, but this weekend is good."

One Friday in late spring, when Kathy was in Cleveland for the bank, I got such a call. I was working on a magazine piece — throwing myself against the four walls of our apartment, really — and Redding was a pleasant place to work (my parents had converted my old bedroom into an office to entice me) so I packed some clothes, toys, my typewriter and a box of notes, picked Seamus up early at the day-care and headed out.

It was a lovely day, and I drove with the windows open. Seamus loved to drive, so once we were out of the city I let him undo his seatbelt and stand on the bench next to me so he could enjoy the passing world. It was a risky arrangement, I knew, but if I hadn't let him do it he would have driven me crazy begging, and after a while he grew bored and sat back down and went to sleep, his neat blonde head wedged like a stone against my thigh, my arm across his back to pull him close. We crossed the miraculous Whitestone, ascended 95 into Connecticut and turned north for Redding, into the heart of a superb green country. We passed a reservoir on which men, playing hooky like myself, sipped cans of beer and fished from cramped, square-bowed prams. Thick trees draped branches over the road like a canopy, and the light sparkled in their leaves as if trapped. My work has taken me all over the world, but never in my experience have I found the right words to capture the uncomplicated beauty of light in trees.

When we got to the house my father was asleep in the recliner in the yellow afternoon light of the den, the paper draped like a tent over his belly. His snoring seemed prearranged to tell me he was alive, for which I was grateful. There was a note on the kitchen door from my mother that said she had gone into the village to stock up on "some things you like." Twice, she had underlined the word *you*. Seamus was groggy and disoriented, so I poured him a glass of milk, made up a plate of Oreos and told him to stay in the kitchen while I unloaded the car.

After, I got a beer from the fridge and took Seamus out to the meadow. This had become a ritual with us; I was trying to teach him to play ball. In a completely inexplicable way, I had supposed he might find a knowledge of softball useful. His hands were still too small for a glove, but he liked to field grounders, which I bunted across the grass to him from a distance of about ten feet. His sense of the game was responsive and sportsmanlike. As I had instructed, he got behind each ball and kneeled to trap it. After he had it in his hands he yelled "coming down," and hurled the ball back to me, often over-throwing or simply sending it straight up, though this rarely discouraged him. His small, loose-limbed body, with features more like his mother's than mine, was another mechanism of the world he was patiently getting to know. We had been playing for close to a half-hour when I heard the slap of a screen door and saw Donny emerge from his parents' house.

He did not look at all well. He walked across the meadow with the halting gait of an old man, and as he approached, I noticed his hair had gone grey. His body, which I had so admired for its robust strength, was wiry and gaunt under his black tee shirt and jeans. Still, he looked like himself.

"Howdy stranger," I said when he was within range.

"Howdy yourself," he called back. Smiling, he put his hand over his brow and peered at my son, who was standing half behind my legs. "Could this be?" he said.

"Seamus, this is Mr. Flannigan." I reached around and nudged my son forward. "Say how-do-you-do."

Donny knelt and looked into my son's face, then up at me. "Jeez, don't I rate an Uncle Donny?"

"Of course. Seamus, this is Uncle Donny. He's an old friend of mine. We used to hang around together."

"How-do-you-do," Seamus recited.

"Glad to know you," Donny said, and enveloped my son's tiny hand with his. "But your father is kidding you. I used to hang around and sometimes let him watch."

"How are your parents?" I asked. "Martha?"

Donny stood and dusted off his hands on the thighs of his jeans. "They're good, Martha is good. She's living in Atlanta now. Of course, I don't know exactly what she does there, but I hear she's good. And you? You're married."

"Sure am," I said, holding up my ring finger. "Almost seven years now."

"Well that's quite a thing," he said, "quite a thing."

For an instant, both of us struggled to find something more to say. It was a difficult silence, but not, to my mind, an embarrassing one; we hadn't seen each other for years, and where did one start? Then we broke it together. "Go ahead," I said.

"No, you," he answered.

"Well, I was just wondering what brings you around," I said.

"College." He smirked, and pushed the hair off his forehead, running his fingers through it like a comb. "Can you believe it? I've got grey hair and I'm still a sophomore in college. I'm finishing up an Associate's Degree at the Community. My parents are letting me live here while I get back on my feet."

"That's great," I offered. There were huge gaps in his history which I could not fill.

"No, it's not great," he said. "Great is ..." he struggled, then tipped his head at Seamus, *"this* is great. But it's a substantial improvement."

"I'm bored," Seamus whined.

"You're always bored," I said, mussing his hair. "Go wake up your grandfather and say hello."

"That's boring," he said. Sometimes he was a stubborn child. "I want to play more."

"Your dad's tired," I said. "Give him a rest, huh?"

"You always did tire easily," Donny said.

"I beg your pardon?"

"You heard me," he said. "The kid wants to play, let's play."

So we did. In a small triangle we tossed the ball back and forth, keeping the conversation directed to Seamus, to what we were doing, which was entertaining my son. I had thought seeing Donny would make me feel nostalgic, but the effect was quite the opposite; playing with my son this way was something totally new.

"Do you remember when you visited me at Silver Lake?" he said after a bit.

"At Silver Lake?" I caught the ball and flipped it off the inner curve of my elbow to Seamus, who nabbed it neatly. Something about having Donny there made us more graceful than usual, afforded us a cleaner, more defined sense of our bodies. "No, I don't think I ever did. I meant to go of course, but I never did."

"I could have sworn," he said, shaking his head as if to unlodge something that had clogged there. "But I suppose I'm really no judge. A lot of things happened back then I'm not so clear on."

I wanted to apologize then — for what, I wasn't sure — but something in the way Donny handled the ball got me past the moment. We played for a while longer, and then I excused myself under the pretense of work and left them and went inside.

My father was awake and making a sandwich in the kitchen. "Where's Shea? You want one?" he asked, offering me his sandwich. "Sorry I was asleep when you came in. I just can't seem to stay awake in the afternoons anymore."

"He's out in the meadow with Donny Flannigan," I said.

What happened next surprised me, not because it was unlikely, but because I just hadn't anticipated it. The plate my father had offered was suddenly spinning on the floor, corned beef and Swiss cheese and slabs of caraway rye scattered like riders hurled from a carnival attraction. At first I thought he was having what he referred to, in moments of theatrical gloom, as "the big one."

"Jesus Christ," he said. "What are you thinking about?"

"They're playing in the meadow, Pop," I said. "It's OK. I left them there."

"You left Seamus out there with that boy? You oughta have your head examined."

"That was years ago, Pop," I said. I reached down to pick up the plate. "And for Christsakes, he's no boy. He's got more grey hairs than you do."

"You don't know what you're talking about."

"Maybe I don't," I said. "But Shea is my son and you can just get it out of your head that you're going out there. I know what you're thinking."

"Oh, yes I am. You bet I am."

I dumped the wreckage in the trash, rinsed off the plate and started making a fresh corned beef and Swiss. "No, you're going to sit down and eat a sandwich and mind your own business. Now, do you want pickles with this or what? I'm not fooling around, Pop."

I knew that behind me he was looking out the window, trying to steal a glance out to the meadow. "I won't do anything," he said. "I'll just go out there and watch, to make sure everything's ok."

I was putting the finishing touches on the sandwich, pinning it together with a couple of toothpicks, just the way he liked it. "I don't believe that for a minute." I handed him the plate, wedging it against his chest so he had to take it. "Just eat this, Pop," I said. "Please. Take the plate. I know what I'm doing."

And I did know, in a general way; when I had Dad down at the table working on his sandwich and was confident he wouldn't go out to the meadow and make a scene, I went up to my office and watched from the window. Donny was kneeling in the dirt, tossing the ball back and forth to Seamus. When the ball passed between them I found myself holding my breath. I could hear Donny saying "attaboy" and "way-to-go," hear Seamus' voice floating like bird-songs across the meadow and up to my window. Then Donny stood up.

"Wanna see something, kiddo?" He lifted the baseball bat off the grass. It was an old Louisville Slugger, twenty years old. As far away as I was, I could see the ancient dents we had cut in the wood, teeing-off on rocks. Donny draped it over his shoulder and set his feet at right angles to the distant line of trees.

"Your father could never do this," he said. Then he tossed the ball up and with a mighty swing — he made the whole thing look effortless, as natural as breathing — blasted it away. From the window I could fully appreciate the dimensional majesty of its arc, as one can best enjoy a homerun from the high boxes of a stadium. It reached the trees thirty feet above the ground and going like a shot. The woods

trembled with the impact. A flock of star-
lings broke loose from the green banks and
gathered in a squawking wheel.

Grey-haired but himself, Donny reclined
on his bat in the attitude of a hale young
slugger. Seamus jumped and clapped,
threw his arms out and wheeled in imita-
tion of the birds. Eventually the chaos in
the woods died down, I heard my mother's
car pull into the drive, and I went out to
gather Seamus and bring him in to his
grandparents.

About the Award

The *National Novella Award* is a prize of $2,500 plus publication given once every two years for the best novella-length work of fiction. Co-sponsored by the Arts and Humanities Council of Tulsa (publisher of *Nimrod* literary magazine) and Council Oak Books, the *National Novella Award* was established in recognition of the novella's increasing popularity and importance in the national culture.

For more information about the National Novella Award competition, write to the Arts and Humanities Council of Tulsa, Inc. at 2210 S. Main, Tulsa, OK 74114.